Ífè Myths
A Collection of Myths of the Yoruba People of Nigeria

By John Wyndham

Revised and Edited By

Dennis Logan

[2021]

Copyright 2021 by Rolled Scroll Publishing
ISBN: 9781952900099

AUTHOR'S NOTE

The author spent several years as an Assistant District Officer among the Yorubas in Nigeria, and was thus enabled to collect the folklore contained in this book from native sources.

The reticence of the natives on religious subjects made it necessary to piece much together from incantations and chance remarks, but it is hoped that the notes will show that no great liberty has been taken with the beliefs of a tribe which inhabits a large area in West Africa.

The legends are bare and uncertain, and it seemed that blank verse would prove a more suitable form to present them than prose.

The author desires to express his indebtedness to Mr. Ford Madox Hueffer for advice when this work was half-finished, and also to the Council of the Royal Anthropological Institute for permission to republish Notes I and XI-XIV which appeared originally in "Man." The suggestions contained in Note IV on the Creation of Man, and in Note VII on the possible connection between the Edi Festival and the Saturnalia, are offered after a subsequent reading of the "Golden Bough."

PERSONS

Arámfè God of Thunder and Father of the Gods.

Orísha Creator of men. Son of Arámfè.

Odúwa or Odudúwa } King of men. Son of Arámfè.

Ógun God of Iron. Son of Odúwa.

Oráyan The warrior son of Ógun.

Ládi Smith of Ógun.

Obálufon A worker in brass.

Mórimi Wife of Obálufon.

Ífa The Messenger of the Gods, principally known by reason of divination.

Olókun Goddess of the Sea.

Olóssa Goddess of the Lagoons.

Óshun A Goddess who transformed and became the River Oshun.

Édi The Perverter. A God of Evil who led men astray.

Éshu	Now regarded as the Devil, but originally as the Undoer of the favours of the Gods.
Peregún 'Gbo	A Forest God who caused the Forest to bring forth wild animals and watched over the birth of Orúnmila.
Orúnmila	A God who watches over the birth of children.
Offun Kánran	A messenger of Ífa.
Órní Odúm'la	The ancestor of the Órnís of Ífè.
Ojúmu	A priest.
Osányi	A priest and maker of charms.

The Sun, Moon, Night, Day, Dawn and Evening were also Gods and Goddesses sent by Arámfè, who is often spoken of as God. But a higher and very distant Being is mentioned by some of the Priests.

Oíbo means White Man.

Okpéllè is a charm used in the divination of Ífa.

The final N is as in bon, and French pronunciation is nearly correct in all the above names.

A white man visits Ífè, the sacred city of the Yórubas, and asks to hear the history of the place. The Órní, the religious head of Yórubaland, begins, and directs the Babaláwo Arába, the chief-priest of Ífa to continue.

I. THE BEGINNING.

The Órní of Ífè speaks:
Oíbo, you have asked to hear our lore,
The legends of the World's young hours—and where
Could truth in greater surety have its home
Than in the precincts of the shrines of Those
Who made the World, and in the mouths of priests
To whom their doings have been handed down
From sire to son?

Arámfè reigns in Heaven;	Before this World was made There reigned Arámfè in the realm of Heaven Amidst his sons. Old were the hills around him; The Sun had shone upon his vines and cornfields Since time past reckoning. Old was Arámfè, The father of the Gods: his youth had been The youth of Heaven... Once when the King reclined Upon the dais, and his sons lay prostrate In veneration at his feet, he spoke
tells his sons of the	Of the great things he purposed: "My sons, you know But fair things which I made for you, before

creation of I called your spirits from the Dusk: for always
Heaven; Your eyes have watched the shadows and the wind
On waving corn, and I have given you
The dances and the chorus of the night—
An age of mirth and sunrise (the wine of Heaven)
Is your existence. You have not even heard
Of the grey hour when my young eyes first opened
To gaze upon a herbless Mass, unshaped
And unadorned. But I knew well the heart
Of Him-Who-Speaks-Not, the far-felt Purpose that gave
Me birth; I laboured and the grim years passed:
Streams flowed along their sunny beds; I set
The stars above me, and the hills about;
I fostered budding trees, and taught the birds
Their song—the unshapely I had formed to beauty,
And as the ages came I loved to make
The beautiful more fair... All went not well:
A noble animal my mind conceived
Emerged in loathsome form to prey upon
My gentle creatures; a river, born to bask
In sunlit channels and mirror the steep hills,
Tore down its banks and ravaged field and plain;

While cataract and jagged precipice,
Now grand with years, remind me of dread days
When Heaven tottered, and wide rifts sundered my young
Fair hills, and all seemed lost. Yet—I prevailed.
Think, now, if the accomplished whole be Heaven,
How wonderful the anxious years of slow
And hazardous achievement—a destiny
For Gods. But yours it has not been to lead
Creation by the cliff's-edge way from Mass
To Paradise." He paused on the remembrance,
And Great Orísha cried: "Can we do naught?
What use in godhead without deeds to do?
Where yearns a helpless region for a hand
To guide it?" And Old Arámfè answered him:

sends them to make the World. "My son, your day approaches. Far-off, the haze
Rests always on the outer waste which skirts
Our realm; beyond, a nerveless Mass lies cold
'Neath floods which some malign unreason heaves.
Odúwa, first-born of my sons, to you I give
The five-clawed Bird, the sand of power.[1] Go now,

---

[1] See Note I on the Creation of the Earth.

Call a despairing land to smiling life
Above the jealous sea, and found sure homesteads
For a new race whose destiny is not
The eternal life of Gods. You are their judge;
Yours is the kingship, and to you all Gods
And men are subject. Wisest of my sons,
Orísha, yours is the grateful task to loose
Vague spirits[2] waiting for the Dawn—to make
The race that shall be; and to you I give
This bag of Wisdom's guarded lore and arts
For Man's well-being and advancement. And you,
My younger sons, the chorus and the dance,
The voice of worship and the crafts are yours
To teach—that the new thankful race may know
The mirth of Heaven and the joys of labour."
Then Odúwa said: "Happy our life has been,
And I would gladly roam these hills for ever,
Your son and servant. But to your command
I yield; and in my kingship pride o'ersteps
Sorrow and heaviness. Yet, Lord Arámfè,
I am your first-born: wherefore do you give

---

[2] See Note IV on the Creation of Man.

> The arts and wisdom to Orísha? I,
> The King, will be obeyed; the hearts of men
> Will turn in wonder to the God who spells
> Strange benefits." But Arámfè said "Enough;
> To each is fitting task is given. Farewell."

The Gods Here the Beginning was: from Arámfè's vales
leave   Through the desert regions the exiled Gods
Heaven. approached
           The edge of Heaven, and into blackness plunged—
           A sunless void o'er godless water lying—[3]
           To seize an empire from the Dark, and win
           Amidst ungoverned waves a sovereignty.

Odúwa   But by the roadside while Orísha slept
steals the   Odúwa came by stealth and bore away
bag and   The bag Arámfè gave. Thus was the will
causes War   Of God undone: for thus with the charmed sand
on Earth.   Cast wide on the unmastered sea, his sons
               Called forth a World of envy and of war.

---

[3] See Note I on the Creation.

        Of Man's Creation, and of the restraint
        Olókun[4] placed upon the chafing sea,
        Of the unconscious years which passed in darkness
        Till dazzling sunshine touched the unused eyes
        Of men, of War and magic—my priest shall tell you,
        And all the Great Ones did before the day
        They vanished to return to the calm hills

Life in Ífè   Of Old Arámfè's realm . . . They went away;
is as it was   But still with us their altars and their priests
in the time   Remain, and from their shrines the hidden Gods
of the Gods   Peer forth with joy to watch the dance they taught,
        And hear each night their chorus with the drum:
        For changeless here the early World endures
        In this first stronghold of humanity,
        And, constant as the buffets of the waves
        Of Queen Olókun on the shore, the song,
        The dance of those old Gods abide, the mirth,
        The life . . . I, too, am born of the Beginning:

---

[4] The Goddess of the Sea.

Odúm'la speaks for the Gods; For, when from the sight of men the Great Gods passed,
They left on Earth Órní Odúm'la[5] charged
To be a father to a mourning people,
To tend the shrines and utter solemn words
Inspired by Those invisible. And when
Odúm'la's time had come to yield the crown,
To wait upon the River's brink,[6] and cross
To Old Arámfè—Ífa,[7] in his wisdom,

and lives for ever in the person of the Órní. Proclaimed that son with whom Odúm'la's soul
Abode. Thus has it ever been; and now
With me that Being is—about, within—
And on our sacred days these lips pronounce
The words of Odudúwa and Orísha.

---

[5] See Note II on Odúm'la, the first Órní of Ílè.
[6] The River which separates this World from the next.
[7] The Messenger of the Gods. See Note XII on his divination.

II. THE DESCENT

Arába speaks:

I am the voice of Ífa, messenger
Of all the Gods: to me the histories
Are known, and I will tell you of the days
Of the Descent. How Old Arámfè sent
The Gods from Heaven, and Odudúwa stole
The bag—my king has told you. . . For many a day
Across unwatered plains the Great Ones journeyed,
And sandy deserts—for such is the stern bar
Set by Arámfè 'twixt his smiling vales

The Gods arrive at the edge of Heaven.
And the stark cliff's edge which his sons approached
Tremblingly, till from the sandy brink they peered
Down the sheer precipice. Behind them lay
The parched, forbidding leagues; but yet the Sun
Was there, and breezes soft, and yet the mountains—
A faded line beyond the shimmering waste—
Called back to mind their ancient home. Beneath
Hung chaos—dank blackness and the threatening roar
Of untamed waters. Then Odudúwa spoke:
"Orísha, what did we? And what fault was ours?

Outcasts to-day; to-morrow we must seek
Our destiny in dungeons, and beneath
That yawning blackness we must found a city
For unborn men. Better a homeless life
In desert places: dare we turn and flee
To some lost valley of the hills? Orísha,
What think you?" Then spoke Orísha whom men call
The Great: "Is this Odúwa that I hear—
My mother's son who stole Arámfè's gift,
And thought to filch away the hearts of men
With blessings which were mine to give? For me,
The arts I know I long to use, and yearn
To see the first of toiling, living men
That I shall make. Forbidding is our task,
You say—but think, ere we return to peace
And Heaven's calm, how boundless is the fate
You flinch from! Besides, is Godhead blind?

You think

Arámfè would not know? Has Might no bodes
With eyes and ears? . . Dumb spirits hungering

Odúwa sends Ojúmu with the Bird,	For life await us: let us go." So spoke Orísha; and Odúwa hung a chain Over the cliff to the dark water's face, And sent Ojúmu, the wise priest, to pour The magic sand upon the sea and loose The five-clawed Bird to scatter far and wide Triumphant land.[8] But, as Earth's ramparts grew, Ever in the darkness came the waves and sucked Away the crumbling shore, while foot by foot Lagoons crept up, and turned to reedy swamps The soil of hope. So Odudúwa called
and Olókun and Olóssa.	Olókun[9] and Olóssa[10] to the cliff And thus he spoke: "Beneath, the waters wrestle With the new-rising World, and would destroy Our kingdom and undo Arámfè's will. Go to the fields of men to be, the homes That they shall make. Olókun! to the sea! For there your rule and your dominion shall be: To curb the hungry waves upon the coastlands

---

[8] See Note I on the Creation of the Earth.
[9] The Goddess of the Sea.
[10] The Goddess of the Lagoons.

For ever. And thus, in our first queen of cities
And secret sanctuaries on lonely shores
Through every æon as the season comes,
Shall men bring gifts in homage to Olókun.
And you, Olóssa, where your ripple laps
The fruitful bank, shan see continually
The offerings of thankful men."

The months

Of Heaven passed by, while in the moonless night

The Bird   Beneath the Bird toiled on until the bounds,
makes the   The corners of the World were steadfast. And then
Earth,   Odúwa called Orísha and the Gods
To the cliff's edge, and spoke these words of sorrow:
"We go to our sad kingdom. Such is the will
Of Old Arámfè: so let it be. But ere
The hour the wilderness which gapes for us
Engulf us utterly, ere the lingering sight
Of those loved hills can gladden us no more—
May we not dream awhile of smiling days
Gone by? . . Fair was drenched morning in the Sun
When dark the hill-tops rose o'er misty hollows;

Fair were the leafy trees of night beneath

The silvering Moon, and beautiful the wind

Upon the grasslands. Good-bye, ye plains we roamed.

The Gods Good-bye to sunlight and the shifting shadows
descend. Cast on the crags of Heaven's blue hills. Ah! wine

Of Heaven, farewell" . . . So came the Gods to Ífè.

Then of an age of passing months untold

By wanings of the Moon our lore repeats

A sunless The dirge of wasting hopes and the lament
World. Of a people in a strange World shuddering

Beneath the thunder of the unseen waves

On crumbling shores around. Always the marsh

Pressed eagerly on Ífè; but ever the Bird

Returned with the unconquerable sand

Ojúmu poured from his enchanted shell,

And the marsh yielded. Then young Ógun bade

The Forest grow her whispering trees—but she

Budded the pallid shoots of hopeless night,

And all was sorrow round the sodden town

Where Odudúwa reigned. Yet for live men

Oríswha creates man.

Orísha, the Creator, yearned, and called
To him the longing shades from other glooms;
He threw their images[11] into the wombs
Of Night, Olókun and Olóssa, and all
The wives of the great Gods bore babes with eyes
Of those born blind—unknowing of their want—
And limbs to feel the heartless wind which blew
From outer nowhere to the murk beyond. . .
But as the unconscious years wore by, Orísha,
The Creator, watched the unlit Dawn of Man
Wistfully—as one who follows the set flight
Of a lone sea-bird when the sunset fades
Beyond a marshy wilderness—and spoke
To Odudúwa: "Our day is endless night,
And deep, wan woods enclose our weeping children.
The Ocean menaces, chill winds moan through
Our mouldering homes. Our guardian Night, who spoke
To us with her strange sounds in the still hours
Of Heaven is here; yet she can but bewail
Her restless task. And where is Evening? Oh! where

---

[11] See Note IV on the Creation of Man.

Is Dawn?" He ceased, and Odudúwa sent
Ífa, the Messenger, to his old sire
To crave the Sun and the warm flame that lit
The torch of Heaven's Evening and the dance...

Arámfè A deep compassion moved thundrous Arámfè,
sends fire, The Father of the Gods, and he sent down
the Sun The vulture with red fire upon his head
and the For men; and, by the Gods' command, the bird
Moon. Still wears no plumage where those embers burned
 him—
 A mark of honour for remembrance. Again
 The Father spoke the word, and the pale Moon
 Sought out the precincts of calm Night's retreat
 To share her watch on Darkness; and Day took wings,
 And flew to the broad spaces of the sky—
 To roam benignant from the floating mists
 Which cling to hillsides of the Dawn—to Eve
 Who calls the happy toilers home.

 And all

The Age Was changed: for when the terror of bright Day
of Mirth. Had lifted from the unused eyes of men,

Sparks flew from Ládi's anvil, while Ógun taught

The use of iron, and wise Obálufon[12]

Made brazen vessels and showed how wine streams out

From the slim palms.[13] And in the night the Gods

Set torches in their thronging courts to light

The dance, and Heaven's music touched the drum

Once more as in its ancient home. And mirth

With Odudúwa reigned.

---

[12] See Note V on Obálufon.

[13] Palm-wine, an efficacious native intoxicant.

III. THE WAR OF THE GODS.

Arába continues:
Oíbo, I will tell and chronicle
A second chapter from the histories

The fable Bequeathed from other times... A tale is told
of Earth, How God in the Beginning sent three sons
Water and Into the World—Earth, Water and the Forest—
Forest With one and twenty gifts for Earth and men
        That are the sons of Earth; and all save one
        The Forest and the Rivers stole; and how
        God promised to his first-born, Earth, that men
        Should win the twenty gifts again by virtue
        Of that last one, Good Humour. And this is true:
        For in those years when Ógun and the Gods
        Made known their handicrafts men learned to seek
        Thatch, food and wine in Forest and in River

Strife Patiently. So Man prevailed; but in those days
between Came strife and turmoil to the Gods—for still
Odúwa For jealousy and pride Odúwa held
        The bag Arámfè gave to Great Orísha.

and   Often Orísha made entreaty; oft
Orísha   A suppliant came before his brother—in vain;
                Till once when Odudúwa sat with Ógun
                In that same palace where the Órní reigns,
                The sound of drums was heard and Great Orísha
                Approached with skilled Obálufon, and said:
                "The time has come to teach Arámfè's arts
                "To men. Give back the bag (for it is mine!)
                That I may do our Father's bidding. Else,
                Have a care, is it not told how caution slept
                In the still woods when the proud leopard fell,
                Lured on by silence, 'neath the monster's foot?"[14]
                Then was Odúwa angered exceedingly:
                "Am I not king? Did not Arámfè make
                Me lord of Gods and men? Begone! Who speaks
                Unseemly words before the king has packed
                His load."[15]

---

[14] cp. Yoruba threat "The Elephant has power to crush the Leopard, though he be silent." (Communicated by drum-beats, I think.)

[15] Yoruba saying. The speaker is probably prepared to travel.

             Orísha and Odúwa called

brings war To arms their followings of Gods and men,
to Ífè.   And on that day the first of wars began
              In Ífè and the Forest. Such was the fall
              Of the Gods from paths divine, and such for men
              The woe that Odudúwa's theft prepared;
              But little the Gods recked of their deep guilt
              Till darkness fell and all was quiet—for then
              Returned the memory of Calm, their heritage,
              Of Heaven born and destined for the World;
              Gloom, too, with the still night came down: a sense
              Of impious wrong, ungodly sin, weighed down
              Warriors aweary, and all was changed. Around,
              Dead, dead the Forest seemed, its boughs unstirred;
              Dead too, amidst its strangling, knotted growth
              The stifled air—while on that hush, the storm's

Arámfè   Mute herald, came the distant thundrous voice
tries to   Of Old Arámfè as he mused: "In vain
stop it;   Into the Waste beneath I sent my sons—
              The children of my happy vales—to make
              A World of mirth: for desolation holds
              The homes of Ífè, and women with their babes

Are outcast in the naked woods." But when
The whirling clouds were wheeling in the sky
And the great trees were smitten by the wind,
Thundrous Arámfè in his ire rebuked
His erring sons: "At my command you came
To darkness, where the Evil of the Void—
Insentient Violence—had made its home,
To shape in the Abyss a World of joy
And lead Creation in the ways of Heaven.
How, then, this brawling? Did the Void's black soul
Outmatch you, or possess your hearts to come
Again into its own? For Man's misfortune
I grieve; but you have borne them on the tide
Of your wrong-doing, and your punishment
Is theirs to share. For now my thunderbolts
I hurl, with deluges upon the land—
To fill the marshes and lagoons, and stay
For aye your impious war."

but fails.   Dawn came; the storm

Was gone, and Old Arámfè in his grief
Departed on black clouds. But still the wrath,
But still the anger of his sons endured,

And in the dripping forests and the marshes
The rebel Gods fought on—while in the clouds
Afar Arámfè reasoned with himself:
"I spoke in thunders, and my deluge filled
The marshes that Ojúmu dried;—but still
They fight. Punish, I may—but what can I
Achieve? In Heaven omnipotent: but here—?
What means it? I cannot tell... In the Unknown,
Beyond the sky where I have set the Sun,
Is He-Who-Speaks-Not: He knows all. Can this
Be Truth: Amidst the unnatural strife of brothers
The World was weaned: by strife must it endure—?"
Oíbo, how the first of wars began,
And Old Arámfè sought to stay the flow
Of blood—your pen has written; but of the days,
The weary days of all that war, what tongue
Can tell? 'Tis said the anger of the Gods
Endured two hundred years: we know the priest
Osányi made strange amulets for all
The mortal soldiers of the Gods—one charm
Could turn a spear aside, a second robbed
The wounding sword of all its sting, another
Made one so terrible that a full score

Must flee—but not one word of the great deeds,
Of hopes and fears, of imminent defeat
Or victory snatched away is handed down:
No legend has defied, no voice called through
The dimness and the baffling years.

But when

An end was come to the ill days foreknown
To Him-Who-Speaks-Not, remembrance of the calm
Of Heaven stole upon the sleepless Gods—
For while the Moon lay soft with all her spell
On Ífè of the many battles; while
With sorrowful reproach the wise trees stood
And gazed upon the Gods who made the soil
The voices of the Forest crooned their dreams
Of peace: "Sleep, sleep" all weary Nature craved,
And "Sleep" the slumbrous reed-folk urged, and 'twixt
The shadow and the silver'd leaf, for sleep

Ógun asks The drowsing breezes yearned. . . . And with the
Odúwa to dawn
give back Ógun, the warrior, with his comrades stood
Before the king, and thus he spoke: "Odúwa,

the bag to Orísha. "We weary of the battle, and its agony
Weighs heavy on our people. Have you forgot
The careless hours of Old Arámfè's realm?
What means this war, this empty war between
One mother's sons? Orísha willed it so,
You say... 'Twas said of old 'Who has no house
Will buy no broom',[16] Why then did Great Orísha
Bring plagues on those he made in love? In Heaven
Afar Arámfè gave to you the empire,
And to Orísha knowledge of the ways
Of mysteries and hidden things. The bag
You seized; but not its clue—the skill, the wisdom
Of Great Orísha which alone could wake
The sleeping lore... The nations of the World
Are yours: give back the bag, and Great Orísha
Will trouble us no more." But neither Ógun
Nor the soft voices of the night could loose
Odúwa from the thrall of envy: the rule
Of men and empire were of no account
When the hot thought of Old Arámfè's lore
Roused his black ire anew. The bag he held;

---

[16] Yoruba saying.

But all the faithless years had not revealed
Its promised treasures. Bitterly he answered:

Odúwa   "These many years my brother has made war
refuses;   Upon his king; while for the crown, its power
And greatness, I have wrought unceasing. To-day
My son—hope of my cause, my cause itself—
Wearies of war, and joins my enemies.
Weak son, the sceptre you were born to hold
And hand down strengthened to a line of kings
Could not uphold your will and be your spur
Until the end. Is it not said, "Shall one
Priest bury, and anon his mate dig up
The corpse?"[17] No day's brief work have you undone,
But all my heart has longed for through a life
Of labour. So let it be: God of Soft Iron!
Upon your royal brow descends this day
The crown of a diminished chieftaincy,
With the sweet honours of a king in name—
For I go back to Old Arámfè's hills

---

[17] Yoruba saying.

and trans-	And the calm realm you prate of." Then Odudúwa
forms to	Transformed to stone and sank beneath the soil,
stone,	Bearing away the fateful bag.
taking the	And thus,
bag with	Beneath, through all the ages of the World
him.	A voiceless lore and arts which found no teacher
	Have lain in bondage.

IV. THE SACRIFICE OF MÓRIMI.[18]

Arába continues:

Oíbo I have told you of the days

When Odudúwa and Orísha fought;

But of the times of peace our annals hold

Strange legends also... Now in the age when mirth

And Odudúwa reigned, grief ever-growing

Befell Great Mórimi, the wife of skilled

Mórimi has no sons, Obálufon—for while his lesser wives

Proudly bore many sons unto their lord,

A daughter only, young Adétoún,

Was granted to his queen. And as the years

Lagged by, a strangeness which he always seemed

To keep in hiding chequered the fair day

With doubtings, and waylaid her in the paths

Of her fond nightly dreams. Once with the Spring,

She saw the clustered tree-tops breaking into leaf

Copper and red and every green, and she

Remembered how beneath the new year's buds

It was ordained by Peregún 'Gbo, lord

---

[18] See Note VI on Mórimi's sacrifice.

Of uninhabitable woods that Life
Should spring from Forest, and Life from Life,—till all
The Woods were gladdened with the voice of beasts
And birds—and thus she reasoned: "Is it not told
How Peregún 'Gbo[19] spoke, and from the womb
Of Forest leaped the sloth that laughs by night?
How 'mid the boughs the sloth brought forth the ape
That bore the leopard? And did not Peregún
Watch o'er the birth of young Orúnmila,
And ever, when the morrow's sorrowing dawn
Must yield up to the leaguing fiends the child's
Fair life, did not the watchful God send down
His messenger to stay the grasping hand
Of Death? Thus do the Gods; and surely one
Will give me sons. Ah! whom must I appease?"

She consults Ífa: Quick with new hope Great Mórimi sought out
A priest of Ífa[20] in his court yard dim,
Where from each beam and smoke-grimed pillar hung
The charms the wise man set to guard his home,

---

[19] See Note XI on Peregún 'Gbo.
[20] See Note XII on the divination of Ífa.

His wives and children from the ills contrived

By the bad spirits. To her gift she whispered,

And laid it on Okpéllè; and the priest

Seizing the charm of Ífa said: "Okpéllè,

To you the woe of Mórimi is known;

You only can reveal its secret cause,

Its unknown cure!" Then he laid down the charm

And Óffun Kánran stood before them. The face

Of Ífa's priest was troubled, and he said:

Who tells her to sacrifice her daughter.

"Mórimi, this is the message of my lord

Ífa: a son, nay many sons, you long for.

You have a daughter, and your husband's love

Was yours. The Gods would give you many sons,

But in your path stands Éshu, the Undoer,

Whose shrine calls out for blood, for sacrifice:

Adétoún." Without hope Mórimi

Went forth, and loathing of the ways of the Gods

Possessed her—while indignation fed her love

Of her one child. . . .

The months passed by: Moons came,

      And in the smiles of happier wives she read
      A mockery; Moons faded from the sky,
      And grief and her Adétoún remained
      Companions of her hours. At last she cried:
      "But sons 1 asked for; I will go again
      And pray for sons and my Adétoún.
      The last word is not yet. Olókun's tide
      Has ebbed: will it not flow again?"

      Yet hope

She   Went not with Mórimi to the dark court
consults Of Ífa's priest; and when a torch disclosed
Ífa again. The self-same bode of sorrow in the dusk—
      To her drear home Great Mórimi fled back
      In terror of the deed which love commanded,
      And love condemned. . . . Silently in the night

Édi   Came Édi, the Perverter, the smooth of tongue,
advises   Who with his guileful reasoning compels
her to act   To conscious sin: "The forms of messengers
on Ífa's   Reveal the thoughts of Ífa, and the ears
message.   Of Ífa, the God-Messenger, have heard
      The far-off, thundrous voice. Would you hold back?

Is not the birth of Nations the first law
Arámfè gave? Can any wife withstand
His will, or maid stern Ógun's call?[21] To-day
Is yours, oh, mother of great kings that shall be:
The green shoots greet the Spring-rain and forget
The barren months, and Mórimi shall know
Her grief and her reproach no more." Then doubt
Seized Mórimi but still she answered; "Will Gods
Not give? Is the grim World a morning market
Where they drive bargains with the folk they made?
Are babes as bangles which Obálufon
Fashions to barter?" But Édi answered her:
"But once Arámfè spoke to Odudúwa,
And with what heavy hearts the Gods went forth
From Heaven's valleys to the blackness! Now thrice,[22]
Thrice to the woman Mórimi the word
Has come—with promise of the World's desire:
Not every wife is chosen for the mother

---

[21] Ógun kills unmarried girls of marriageable age.

[22] According to the legend, Mórimi consulted Ífa three times before acting on his advice.

Of a house of kings. And think!—Obálufon!"
Then Édi, the Perverter, hid his form
In darkness; and with the dawn a young girl lay

The death On the Undoer Éshu's altar—while
of Adétoún. The lazy blue of early morning smoke
Crept up the pass between the hills.

V. THE ÚBO WARS.[23]

Arába continues:

After the	Oíbo, graven on my memory
War of the	Is the sad legend which my father told me
Gods, Ífè	Of the Great Gods' departure... The years slid by
returns	Unnoted while King Ógun[24] reigned. The World
to the arts	Was young: upon the craggy slopes the trees
of peace.	Shot forth red buds, and ancient Ífè, gaunt
	With suffering, dreamed again her early dreams.
	Taught by the Gods, the folk began to learn
	The arts of Heaven's peace anew; the drum
	Returned to measures of the dance, and Great
	Orísha saw the joy of life once more
	In his creatures' eyes. Thus lived mankind among
The	The Gods, and multiplied until the youth
foundation	Of Ífè sought new homes and wider lands
of Úbo	In the vast Forest; and thus was born the first
	Fair daughter of Odúwa's city. Men called

---

[23] See Note VII on Úbo and the Édi Festival.
[24] See Note X on Ógun.

               Her Úbo, and the leader took the name
               Olúbo of Úbo with his chieftaincy.

is attended But to these colonists the Gods, their Fathers,
by strife   Gave no good gifts: 'midst battles with the Wild,
from the   'Mid struggles with the Forest the town grew—
first.   While dull remembrance of unnatural wrongs
               Bred Man's first rebel thought against the Gods;
               And when the time of festival was near,
               Word came to Ífè that the folk of Úbo
               Would bring no gifts, nor worship at the feet
               Of Ógun. But the King scorned them, laughing:
               "Who lights
               His lamp between the leopard's paws?"[25]

The Chief Years passed

of Úbo   In grieving while Olúbo sought the homes
seeks advice, Of spirits of the Forest springs, laid gifts
               At crossway shrines where childless women go,
               Or wandered to drear coasts to share his wrongs
               With Ocean chafing at his old restraint.
               But rivers answered not, not brooks, nor Gods

---

[25] Yoruba saying.

Of crossway altars at the light of dawn;
And through the unceasing hissing of the foam
No voice of counsel came... With Autumn's fall
Olúbo came with gifts before the shrine
Of the grim Forest-God who hedged his land,
And prayed him to accept the corn he brought
And the fat beasts, nor seize his lands again.
And the God saw the oil, and smelled the blood
Of birds and cattle; and the longed-for voice

which the Came to Olúbo: "See with the rain I come
Forest-God Each year upon your fields with springing trees,
gives him Rank-growing grass and vegetation wild:
Your work of yester-year is all undone
By my swift desolation. Be this your symbol:
Go thus against the Scornful Ones arrayed
As I."

In Ífè was great joy: the last

Black thundercloud has passed; the maids were wed,
And all men feasted on the sacred days

Olúbo in- Of Ógun and the Lord of Day—when sudden,
vades Ifè, From the still Forest o'er the walls there broke

and takes the men away as slaves.	Portents of moving trees and hurrying grass On Ífè's stone-still revellers. (Hope perishes In the dark hour a mother sees the dance Of white-robed goblins[26] of the midnight streets— A glimpse, no more; and her sick child is lost). Despair held rule: the new-wed wives were lone; Their men were slaves of Úbo lords. The drum Was silent, and laughter mute. About dull tasks A listless people wandered; but not so
Mórimi consults Ífa,	Mórimi—for she, assured of triumph, strode To the dim court of Ífa, and laid bare Her gift. A vision flickered and was gone, And the priest prophesied: "The bode is good. As when a sick man lies beset by fiends[27] I call not to the Gods for aid, but take The pepper on my tongue and thus invoke Those very fiends in their dread mother's name, And then command the Prince of leaguing Woes (Though hastening to the River's lip) to turn

---

[26] See Note XIII. These goblins are called Elérè.
[27] See Note XIII for the incantation.

              Again—such now is Ífa's counsel, borne
              Swift in the form of Messengers to me

who advises His priest, his voice: 'Evil has come down on Ífè:
her to go   By Evil only can desire prevail.
to Úbo.   Take six he-goats to Éshu, the Undoer;
              Thus crave his aid and go, Great Mórimi,
              A harlot to the land of Úbo'" . . So sped
              Mórimi to the rebel town; and when

She finds   A lord of Úbo sought her midst the shades
out the   Of night, the Undoer's will possessed his lips,
secret.   And he betrayed the way of Úbo's downfall.
              While Éshu's shrine yet ran with blood, the Gods,

Meanwhile, Unknowing, sat alone in their abasement,
the gods   And Ógun said: "We scorned our upstart son;
transform   Scorned him and let him be—nor bore in mind
to stones,   The wisdom of the Past, 'A little snake
rivers,   Is yet a snake.'[28] See now the end has come:
etc.,   Swift from the sight of mocking men we must
              Depart. The sage Osányi will lay wide
              The door of our deliverance: come then—

---

[28] Yoruba saying.

                For naked of dominion what are we Gods?"
                And one by one Osányi gave his charms
                To the lorn Gods. . Orísha could but moan
                "Children I made you—who but I?" and sank
                Beneath the soil he loved. And Óshun[29] threw
                Her body down—but never ceased: a stream
                Gushed up, the sacred stream that flows for ever.
                Olókun[30] fell; 'neath the wide Earth she flowed
                To the broad spaces of her troubled realm. . .

except   So went the Gods; but last, as Osányi gave
Ógun.   The charm to Ógun, last of all the Gods—
                Back from the rebel town Great Mórimi
                Rushed back, and cried: "The fire the vulture brought
                Shall slay the hosts of Úbo!". . . The months crept by
                Fate-laden, white King Ógun's warrior son,

Orányan   Orányan,[31] schooled the sireless lads to War;
destroys   But when the festive season came, he hid
                Them with red fire prepared within the city,

---

[29] See Note VIII on Óshun.

[30] See Note IX on Olókun.

[31] See Note X on Ógun and Orányan.

the Úbo army.	And, as the invading hosts of Úbo scaled
	The walls, a rush of flaming boughs destroyed
	Grass garments and rebellious men. Thus fell
	Úbo before Orányan, and her folk
	Saw slavery in Ífè. . .
	Time spared these deeds—
	But gave to the impenetrable wilds
	The place where Úbo stood, her rebel Gods,
The Édi Festival	Her rites. And here in Ífè, by command
	Of Mórimi, the children of the captives
	Worship Olúbo, but must flee before
	Orányan's fire. And on those days of feasting
	No man may blame his wife for her misdeeds—
	All-mindful of the guile of Mórimi.

VI. THE PASSING OF ÓGUN.

Arába continues:

After the
Úbo Wars,
Ógun
reigns

in peace.

    An age passed by, and Ífè knew no more
    Of battles; for Ógun, grey and bent, chose out
    The way of peace beloved of Old Arámfè.

        Forgotten lives were lived, and shadowy priests
        Kept warm the altars of the departed Gods:
        Old men went softly to the River's lip[32]
        Unsung: 'twixt hope and fear mute colonists
        Went forth to the strange forests of the World;
        And unremembered wives sought out the shrines
        Of the givers of new life. Their names are lost. . .

        Yet now, Oíbo, let a final tale
        Be told; for, at the last, that silent age

---

[32] The River which separates this World from the next.

Yields up the legend of its fall. In those
Last tranquil years the mothers blessed King Ógun
For peaceful days and night's security;
And old men used to tell of their brave deeds
In battles where Oranyan led, applaud
The torch-lit dance and pass their last calm days
Happily... But then came traders from the wilds
By thorn and tangle of scarce-trodden ways
Through the dim woods with wondrous tales they heard
At crossway markets[33] in far lands of deeds
Oranyan did on battlefields beyond
The region of the forests. These tales, oft-told
In house and market, filled the air with rumours
And dreams of war which troubled the repose
Of ancient Ífè—for, while the fathers feared
The coming of the day when the grey God,
Aweary of Earth's Kingship, would go back
To his first far-off home, the young men's dreams
Were always of Oranyan, and their pale days

---

[33] Markets are often found at crossroads in the forest.

Orányan   Lagged by. . . Such were the various thoughts of men
returns   In Ífè, when on a clay, unheralded,
from   Orányan[34] with a host appeared before
distant   Her peaceful gates. None could deny his entrance:
Wars to   The hero strode again the streets he saved
demand the From the Olúbo's grass-clad men, and came
crown.   Before his father to demand the crown
                Of Odudúwa. King Ógun spoke: "My son,
                'Tis long since you were here, and you are welcome.
                But why with these armed men do you recall
                Times well-forgotten and the ancient wars?
                This is a land of peace: beneath the shade
                Of Ífè's trees the mirth of Heaven's vales
                Has found a home, the chorus and the dance
                Their measure. Lay by your arms, and may no hurt
                Attend your coming or your restful hours!"
                Harshly Orányan answered his old father:
                "You speak of peace, Great Ógun, and the calm
                Arámfè destined for a World to be.
                Arámfè spoke—and Odudúwa's dream
                Of wisdom linked to supreme power begat

---

[34] See Note X. on Ógun and Orányan.

A theft!³⁵ And that same night on Heaven's rim
Devised another destiny for men.
What Heaven-sent art has Ógun to undo
That deed, and bid the still-born live? Besides,
Who taught the peaceful peoples of the World
Their longing for red War? Who forged their weapons—
With steel Arámfè gave for harvesting?
Who slew young maids who would not wed to bear
More sons for ancient wars? Who, pray, but Ógun,
The God of War? . . What then? 'Tis said: 'The field
The father sowed his son shall reap!'"³⁶ And Ógun
Made answer: "The story of my life has been
As the succeeding seasons in the course
Where Óshun pours her stream. First, long ago,
The sunny months of heaven when I roamed
A careless boy upon the mountains; then,
As a whole season when the boisterous storms
Fill full the crag-strewn bed with racing waters,
And the warm Sun is hidden by the clouds,

---

³⁵ The theft of Orísha's bag.
³⁶ Yoruba saying.

Doom brought me journeys, toils in darkness, wars
And yet more wars. Again the barren months
Are here: the wagtail lights upon the rock
The river hid; a lazy trickle moves
And in my age Arámfè's promised peace
Gives back her stolen happiness to Ífè. . . .
And now, the sage Osányi[37] is no more,
His charms forgotten: I cannot turn to stone
And vanish like Odúwa; I cannot cast
My worn old body down to rise instead
A river of the land, as Óshun did.
No, Earth must hold me, glad or desolate,
A King or outcast in the vague forest,
Till Heaven call me—when the locked pools bask,
And Óshun sleeps. . . Till then I ask to be
In peace; and, with my tale of days accomplished,
My last arts taught, Arámfè's bidding done—
I, the lone God on Earth who knows fair Heaven,
And the calm life the Father bade us give
To men,—I, Ógun, will make way, and go
Upon the road I came." But Orányan said:

---

[37] Osányi made the charms which enabled the Gods to transform.

"Let the first Mistress of the World decide.
These years the kingly power has passed away
From the old sleeping town Odúwa built
To me, Oranyan, battling in far lands
Where no voice spoke of Ífè. Let Ífè choose
Her way: obscurity or wide renown!"
    A silence fell: the black clouds of the storm
Were overhanging human destiny;
The breathless pause before the loud wind's blast
Held all men speechless—though they seemed to heave

The old men desire Ógun to remain;   For utterance. At length, Eléffon, the friend
Of Ógun, voiced the fond hopes of the old chiefs
Who feared Oranyan and his coming day:
"Ours is the city of the shrines which guard
The spirits of the Gods, and all our ways
Are ordered by the Presences which haunt
The sacred precincts. The noise of war and tumult
Is far from those who dream beneath the trees
Of Ífè. There is another way of life:
The way of colonists. By God's command,
From this first breast the infant nations stray

To the utter marches of humanity.
Let them press onward, and let Orányan lead them
Till the far corners of the World be filled;
Let the unruly fall before their sword
Until the Law prevail. But let not Ífè
Swerve from the cool road of her destiny
For dreams of conquest; and let not Ógun leave
The roof, the evening firelight and the ways
Of men—to go forth to the naked woods."
And the old chiefs echoed: "Live with us yet, Oh,
Ógun!
Reign on your stable throne." But murmurs rose

but the From the young men—suppressed at first, then
young men louder—
acclaim Until their leader, gaining courage, cried:
Orányan. "Empty our life has been—while from far plains,
Vibrant with the romance, the living lustre,
Orányan's name bestows, great rumours came
To mock our laggard seasons; and each year
Mórimi's festival recalls alike
The hero's name and Ífè's greatness. Must
All Ífè slumber that the old may drowse?

No; we will have Orányan, and no other,
To be our King." And a loud cry went up
From his followers: "Orányan is our King!"
And in that cry King Ógun heard the doom
A chieftain of our day sees clear in eggs[38]
Of fateful parrots in his inmost chamber:
The walls of his proud city (his old defence)
Can never more uphold a rule of iron
For victor treachery within. And wearily
He spoke his last sad words: "My boyhood scarce
Had ended on Arámfè's happy hills
When I came here with Odudúwa; with him,
Lovingly I watched this ancient city growing,
And planted the grand forests for a robe
For queenly Ífè. I have grown old with Ífè:
Sometimes I feel that Ógun did become
Ífè, and Ífè Ógun, with the still lapse

---

[38] A gift of parrot's eggs to a Yoruba chief is an intimation that he has reigned long enough and that, should he die by his own hand, trouble would be saved.

Ógun goes away. Of years. Yet she rejects me. Ah! my trees
Would be more kind, and to my trees I go."

    Dawn came; and Ógun stood upon a hill
To Westward, and turned to take a last farewell
Of his old queen of cities—but white and dense,
O'er harbouring woods and unremembering Ífè
A mist was laid and blotted all. . Beyond,
As islands from a morning sea, arose
Two lone grey hills; and Ógun dreamed he saw
Again those early days, an age gone by,
When he and Great Odúwa watched the Bird
Found those grand hills with magic sand,—bare slopes,
Yet born to smile. . . That vision paled: red-gold
Above grey clouds the Sun of yesterday
Climbed up—to shine on a new order. . So passed
Old Ógun from the land.

NOTES

I. THE CREATION.

The relationships of the various gods are differently stated by different chiefs and priests of Ífè, and also by the same men at different times.

It appears, however, that Arámfè ruled in Heaven, and sent his sons, Odúwa and Orísha, to a dark and watery region below to create the world and to people it. According to the legends told in Ífè, the gods were not sent away as a punishment; but there is some story of wrong-doing mentioned at Ówu in the Jébu country. Arámfè gave a bag full of arts and wisdom to Orísha, and the kingship to Odúwa.

On the way from Heaven Odúwa made Orísha drunk, and stole the bag. On reaching the edge of Heaven, Odúwa hung a chain over the cliff and sent down a priest, called Ojúmu, with a snail-shell full of magic sand and a "five-fingered" fowl. Ojúmu threw the sand on the water and the fowl kicked it about. Wherever the fowl kicked the sand, dry land appeared. Thus the whole world was made, with Ífè as its centre.

When the land was firm, Odúwa and Orísha let themselves down the chain, and were followed by several other gods. Orísha began making human beings; but all was dark and cold, because Arámfè had not sent the sun with Odúwa. So Odúwa sent up, and Arámfè sent the sun, moon and fire. (Fire was sent on a vulture's head, and that is why the vulture has no feathers on its head.) Then the gods began to teach their arts and crafts to men.

After many years Orísha made war upon Odúwa to get back his bag. The various gods took sides, but some looked on. The medicine-men provided amulets for the men on both sides. Arámfè was angry with his sons for fighting and threw his thunderbolts impartially—for he was the god of thunder in those days. The war is said to have lasted 201 years, and came to an end only because the gods on Odúwa's side asked him to give back the bag. Odúwa, in a huff, transformed to stone and sank beneath the earth, taking the bag with him. His son, Ógun, the god of iron, then became king.

II. ODÚM'LA, THE FIRST ÓRNÍ OF ÍFÈ

According to tradition, when the gods transformed, they ordered Odúm'la to speak for them, to be a father to the whole world and to remain on Earth for ever. In the words of an old chief: "It is our ancient law that the spirit of Odúm'la passes from body to body, and will remain for ever on the earth. The spirits of the gods are in their shrines, and Odúm'la speaks for them "

I think the Órní claims to be Odúm'la himself. This is a matter of dogma, and I express no opinion.

III. ODÚWA.

There is little to add to the story of Odúwa told in Parts I, II & III.

Arába told me another version of the end of the War of the Gods: Orísha and Odúwa agreed to stop the fighting on condition that each should have a man for sacrifice every seven months. Fourteen months was then regarded as a year.

Another story Arába told me was: "The Moon is a round crystal stone, which is with Odúwa. They take it in front when they go to sacrifice to Odúwa—otherwise the god would injure the man who offers the sacrifice." Odúwa is said to have taken the stone from a Moslem, and to have been in the habit of looking at it.

When I went to Odúwa's shrine, there was a great knocking of doors to warn the god of my arrival. I did not see the stone.

IV. ORÍSHA AND THE CREATION OF MAN.

The legend of Orísha's creation of Man is mysterious. He is said to have thrown images into wombs. I was once told he put signs into women's hands. I can only account for this story by the suggestion that it may date from a period when men had not discovered the connection between sexual intercourse and the birth of children.

As to spirit life before birth, the priest of Arámfè said "A child may have been with the spirits, but when he is born he forgets all about it."

The sacrifice offered to Orísha consists of eight goats, eight fishes, eight rats and eight kola-nuts.

Orísha was a god of great knowledge (apart from the contents of the bag which was stolen from him), and taught his son, Oluorógbo—who, according to tradition, is the ancestor of the white races.

The Órní attributes ascendancy of Europeans to the up-bringing of Oluorógbo.

Our ancestor has need of eggs, fowls, sheep, kola—and snails.

V. OBALUFON.

Little is told of Obálufon, the husband of Mórimi.

He was a man sent from Heaven by Arámfè, and was a weaver and a worker in brass. He also showed the people how to tap the palms for palm-wine.

Apart from that, "he took care of everybody as a mother of a child, and used to go round the town to drive out sickness and evil spirits."

His image represents him as a king.

VI. MÓRIMI.

Mórimi is the great heroine of the Ífè legends. The story of her sacrifice which I have adopted is Arába's version.

I went also to Mórimi's priest, who showed me her image—of painted wood and no artistic merit—representing a naked negress. His story was much the same as Arába's; but, in his version, Mórimi sacrificed her only son, Yésu, for the whole world and not to any god. It would appear that some early Christian missionary had recognised the Virgin Mary in Mórimi; but it may be doubted whether the missionary had heard of Mórimi's visit to Úbo (See Note VII).

VII. ÚBO AND THE ÉDI FESTIVAL.

The story of the Úbo Wars is that some colonists went from Ífè to found a new town which they called Úbo; but as the Gods had given them nothing, they invaded Ífè. On the first occasion they were driven back; but the next year they came dressed in grass, terrified the people of Ífè and took the men as slaves. (And in those parts of Africa dead kings and gods in need of sacrifice are believed to prefer slaves to free men).

Then Mórimi consulted Ífa, and was told to sacrifice six goats and six bags of cowries to Éshu, and go as a harlot to Úbo. Her mission was successful, and she returned with the necessary information—only to find the gods had transformed to rivers, stones, etc. (It seems that Ógun did not transform, as he was afterwards displaced by his son, Oránynn).

Acting on Mórimi's advice, Oránynn set fire to the Úbo soldiers on their next inroad.

The end of Úbo is commemorated by Édi (the festival of Mórimi, which began on the 21st November in 1913). Men dressed in hay parade the town, but have to run for their lives when others pursue them with fire. Fire is also taken out to the Bush.

On the first day of Édi, the Órní appears, but must remain in the Afin (Palace) for the remaining seven. During this period the women do honour to Mórimi's share in the victory by emulating her deed, and their husbands are not allowed to interfere.

The meaning of the legend is doubtful. There may have been such a town as Úbo, but it seems likely that the Festival is connected with agriculture.

Úbo (or Ígbo) means the Bush, and Mórimi may have advised the customary burning of the Bush to prepare the land for crops. The date of the Festival (early in the dry season), the fire and the men dressed in hay, all suggest this interpretation. On the other hand, the same arguments, combined with the seclusion of the Órní and the license of the women, would favour the view that Édi was the more general Festival of the Saturnalia. Possibly it was so originally; and the demons to be driven out appeared so material in the form of tropical vegetation that Úbo (the Bush to be burned) has obscured the former meaning of the Festival. If this be so, Mórimi's mission to Úbo may be a later fable to account for the license of the women before farming operations begin.

VIII. OSHUN.

Óshun was a woman (or goddess) in high favour with both Odúwa and Orísha. "It were well were Óshun with us," said Odúwa, and Orísha agreed. Accordingly she took her place on Odúwa's left, Orísha being on his right; that is to say Óshun was considered the third personage in Ífè.

The second chief in Ífè, the Obalúfe, claims descent from Óshun for himself and half the people of his quarter of the town. He has a well in his compound, called Óshun, which is said to be the actual water into which Óshun transformed herself. He says his first forefather took a calabash of the water with him when he went to war, and this gallon became the source of the River. The source is forty miles from Ífè, and perhaps the Obalúfe is right. The well is never dry; and it is needless to add that the water has many curative properties. One would be surprised if a descendant of Óshun died, except from other causes.

"At the time of the Óshun Festival," says Obalúfe, "all her tribe collect sheep, goats, yams, agidi, palm-wine, kola, rats, fish and pigeons, and bring them to me for the feast. Óshun gets the blood of goats, sheep and pigeons, the head of a rat—but not of a fish. We eat the fish—although they are the children of Óshun and consequently our brothers." Óshun is more strait-laced than her descendants.

IX. OLÓKUN

There is a pond in Ífè called Ókun (the Ocean), where Olókun transformed to water. Thence she flowed underground, and came out in the sea.

Her priest showed me a bronze head of Olókun, which has considerable merit. He told me that, in return for sacrifice, Olókun gives beads. In Benin, Olókun is considered to be the Goddess of Wealth as well as of the Sea; and a King of Benin, who must have been alive about 1400 A.D., is said to have found the treasures of Olókun laid out on the shore and to have looted her coral.

X. OGUN AND ORANYAN

Ógun was the son of Odúwa, and is usually regarded as the God of Iron and of War.

According to his chief-priest (the Oshógun), he went away to war and captured a woman called Deshóju, whom he made his wife. When Ógun returned to Ífè, Odúwa took Deshóju from his son. There is therefore some doubt as to whether Ógun was the father of Orányan—who was born with a leg, an arm and half his body black, the remainder being white (according to the Oshógun).

Ógun may have had other attributes. He may have been a Phallic Deity, because there are hewn stones in Ífè, called the staves of Ógun, which appear to be of Phallic origin. It is also noteworthy that, at the time of his Festival, Ógun is said to kill any marriageable girl he may find in her mother's house. (This happened once to Arába; the prospective son-in-law could not produce £5, and Arába, who gives no credit, lost a potential five pound note in the shape of his daughter). Further, when a child is circumcised the severed skin is put in a calabash of Ógun "to worship him (together with a snail in order that the wound may heal)."

Ógun may also have been the Sun-God (or a worshipper of the Sun-God). His festival is commonly called Olójjor (Lord of Day). Oshogun says Ógun was Olójjor; Arába says Olójjor was someone else, the confusion being due to the circumstance that the two festivals take place at the same time. In this connection, the half-and-half colouring of Orányan is suggestive.

The dog is the principal animal used for sacrifice to Ógun. Orán018 prefers a ram, a rat, kola and much palm-wine.

Eventually, Orányan displaced his father, who planted his staves in Ífè and went away. I have presumed the death of Osányi, as I cannot otherwise explain the fact that Ógun "went away" instead of transforming as the other gods had done. In his turn, Orányan "went away: he had too much medicine to die."

XI. THE CULT OF PEREGÚN 'GBO.

Peregún 'Gbo (or Peregún Ígbo) seems to have been a god who caused the forest to bring forth birds and beasts. He was a son of God, and came to earth with Ebbor (worship) and Édi, a god who causes men to do what they know to be wrong.

It is evident from the incantation below that Peregún 'Gbo was originally approached by people in need of children, but nowadays the same formula is recited by the priest whatever a man may be asking for. The priest tells the man to bring a sheep, kola, palm-oil, a pigeon, a cock, and a hen; also a live goat for the priest.

The priest kills the sheep, pigeon, cock and hen. The three birds and a part of the sheep are placed in separate broken pots with palm-oil. The man is then told to produce nine pennyworth of kowries, which are also put in the pots. The priest takes the balance of the mutton in addition to the live goat. The priest then faces the pots, puts pepper (átarè) into his mouth, and recites the incantation:—

1. *Ígbo lóbi íror*
    The forest bore the sloth.

2. *Íror lóbi ógubor*
    The sloth bore the monkey.

3. *Ógubor lóbi áhan-námajá*
   The monkey bore the leopard.

4. *Ahan-námajá lóbi érelu-agáma*
   The leopard bore the guinea-fowl.

5. *Érelu-agáma lóbi ekusá*
   The guinea-fowl bore the hawk.

6. *Ékusá lóbi óju-gbona*
   The hawk bore the evil spirit who guards Heaven's gate.

7. *Óju-gbona lóbi áfi íkere-tíkere éhin éku.*
   The evil spirit bore the generative organs of men and women.

8. *Peregún 'Gbo ni abobá Imálè.*
   Untranslated. Imale is Peregún 'Gbo's messenger and is sent to do what the man asks.

9. *Oriyámi la-popo*
   Good luck is human.

10. *Ése ámi lápè okúte ába*
    The father of a lucky child is lucky.

11. *Atorladórla Igbadá lordífa fun Orúnmila nigbatí nwon fi ojor íku re dóla.*
    Atorladorla Igbadá approached Ífa on behalf of Orúnmila when they had fixed his death for the morrow. (Atorladórla Igbadá is a good spirit who keeps on postponing an evil deed contemplated by someone.)

12. *Orúnmila ni kátikun tíkun kátikerè tikerè.*
    Orúnmila says menstruation will cease, and pregnancy will begin.

13. *Orúnmila ni on ko yúnle orun.*
    Orúnmila says that he (the child) will not go to Heaven (*i.e.* will be born alive).

When the priest has finished the recitation, the man takes the pots to the shrine of Éshu (the Devil). The first ten sentences are in praise of Peregún 'Gbo, who ordered Atorladórla Igbadá to go to Ífa, and is now asked to send Imále to Orúnmila with the applicant's request. (The incantation is apparently in some form of archaic Yoruba, and the Babaláwo had to explain much of it to the interpreter. Some of the translations are probably very loose).

XII. THE DIVINATION OF ÍFA (A FRAGMENT)

Ífa was the Messenger of the Gods, and is consulted by the Yoruba on all subjects.

His priests (called Babaláwo) profit considerably by divination, which they perform with sand on a circular board, or with a charm called Okpéllè.

Okpéllè consists of eight pieces of bark on a string. These eight are arranged in fours.

Each of the pieces of bark may fall either with the outside or the inside showing. Consequently each set of four may fall in sixteen different ways having different names and meanings.

The sixteen names are:—

1. Ógbè—all face down—inside showing.

2. Oyéku—all face up—outside showing.

3. Iwóri.

4. Édi.

5. Obára.

6. Okánran.

7. Róshun.

8. Owórin.

9. Égutan.

10. Ossa.

11. Eréttè.

12. Etúrah.

13. Ológbon.

14. Ékka.

15. Oshé.

16. Offun or Orángun.

When Okpéllè is thrown on the ground and the two fours are identical the resultant is called:—

Ogbe Meji (*i.e.* Two Ogbes)	Egutan Meji
Oyeku Meji	Ossa Meji
Iwori Meji	Erétte Meji
Édi Meji	Eturah Meji
Obára Meji	Ologbon Meji
Okánran Meji	Ekka Meji
Roshun Meji	Oshe Meji, or
Aworin Meji	Offun Meji

These are called the Sixteen Messengers of Ífa.

The chance, however, of the four on the Babaláwo's left agreeing with that on his right is only one in sixteen. The other fifteen combinations which may appear with Ogbe on the right are called: Ogbe Yeku, Ogbe Wori, Ogbe Di, &c., similarly with the other Messengers of Ífa. These combinations are called the children of the

Messenger who appears on the right. Thus, Ogbe Yeku is a child of Ogbe; Oyeku Logbe is a child of Oyeku.

From this it will be seen that Okpéllè can show 256 combinations.

Procedure.—A man comes to a Babaláwo to consult Ífa. He places a gift of cowries (to which he has whispered his needs) before the Babaláwo. The latter takes Okpéllè and places it on the cowries. He then says: "You, Okpéllè, know what this man said to the cowries. Now tell me." Then he lifts Okpéllè and lays it out on the floor. From the messenger or child which appears the Babaláwo is supposed to deduce that his client wants a son, has stolen a goat, or has a toothache, as the case may be. He then tells him what he must bring as a sacrifice to achieve his ends. In all cases the sacrifice (or a large part of it) is offered to Éshu (the devil) for fear that he might undo the good work. For instance, the client is poor and needs money: Édi Méji appears, and the Babaláwo tells his client to bring a dog, a fowl, and some cowries and palm-oil. The man splits the dog and the fowl; puts palm-oil and cowries inside them, and takes them to Éshu. The Babaláwo presumably takes the bulk of the cowries for himself.

The appearance of Ógbe Méji promises long life, but a goat must be brought.

If a man has no children and Oyéku Méji appears, he must bring a ram and a goat.

Iwóri Méji demands eggs, a pigeon, and cowries from a sick man.

Édi Méji.—As above.

Obára Méji.—A sacrifice of 2 cocks, 2 hens, and 250 cowries is needed to purify after menstruation.

Okánran Méji.—A goat and 500 cowries bring on menstruation.

Róshun Méjí.—A she-goat and 2 hens to cure a headache.

Awórin Méji.—4 cocks and 800 cowries to bring about the death of one's enemy.

Égutan Méji.—A ram (large) and 1,200 cowries to cure a bad bellyache.

Ossa Méji.—Butcher's meat and 4 pigeons to drive away witchcraft.

Erétte Méji.-2 pigeons, 2 cocks, and 600 cowries to get children.

Etúrah Méji.—One large gown, a, sheep, and 300 cowries to cure eye disease.

Ológbon Méji.—Sacrifice 4 snails and 4 pigeons if you suspect someone wishes to poison you.

Ekka Méji.—4 hens, oil, and 700 cowries for earache.

Offun Méji.—If children keep on dying, sacrifice 16 snails, 16 rats, 16 fishes, and 1,600 cowries, and the following children will live.

Osse Méji.—8 snails, 8 pigeons, and 800 cowries for children.

Ogbe Yeku.—(a) If a man has no money, he must bring 4 pigeons, 2 shillings, and soap. The Babaláwo mixes leaves (*ewe-ire*) with the soap as a charm, and the man must use it for a bath.

(b) If a man is very ill, he must offer 3 he-goats and 5s. 6d. He will then be better.

Ogbe Wori.—(a) If a man is sick, he must offer 8s. and a sheep. Otherwise he will die.

(b) If a man needs money, he must bring thread and 6 pigeons and buy soap. The Babaláwo gets *ewe aji* and puts them on the soap with the pigeon's blood. The thread is put inside the soap. The man then washes.

(c) If a man has committed a crime, he must bring 7 cocks and 35s. The Babaláwo kills the cocks, and takes the 35s. for himself. He takes the sand of Ogbe Wori from the Ífa board and puts some on each cock's breast, with 260 cowries. Five of the cocks are then given to Éshu and the other 2 are taken to a place where three roads meet. Then either a necessary witness will not appear in court or the accused will be found not guilty.

(d) If two men want the same woman, and Ogbe Wori appears (when one of them consults Ífa), the Babaláwo asks for 4 hens and a he-goat. The woman then becomes the client's wife. Éshu gets the hens and the goat's blood; the Babaláwo, the goat.

XIII. A CURE FOR SUDDEN AND SERIOUS ILLNESSES.

The priest puts pepper (atáre) into his mouth and recites:—

Akélejá! Akélejá!
A spirit who grips a man by the throat and makes breathing quick and uneasy.

Akélewóssa!
A spirit who causes eye-disease.

Akútobárun!
Spirits which trouble sick persons.

Amúrorfáshorgérrè!
Spirits now called Anjánu, who cause delirium.

Amulepásheyé!
One who causes bad bellyache.

Ojobolóro!
   Spirits who cause severe headaches.

Abiyéte-ashórmunyányan!
   One "who has a very sharp edge to his cloth," and causes backache.

Asá-ntétè-mofárapá!
   Imps seen at night in white cloths. Now called Elérè. They afflict children.

Olómo-áro, niyéye éshukú!
   "Olómo-áro, who art the mother of evils." She does no harm but is invoked because her children, already named, will listen when prayed in their mother's name.

Arónposhé Íreké!
   The husband of Olómo-áro and the father of the evil spirits. If he is not invoked the sick man dies. He is also called upon to stop his sons' mischief.

Íshuku den lényimi!
   "Evil, leave my back!" When this has been spoken, the spirits leave the sick man.

Bi Ébura Nla ba de éti ómi, apéyinda.
   "If the Great Evil comes to the river's bank, he will turn back."

Ébura Nla is the master of all the evils. If called by the other spirits, he comes to the further bank of the river Arénkenken, which is described as the "water of Heaven". If he crosses to the near side, the sick man dies.

After finishing the incantation, the priest takes some of the pepper from his tongue and puts in on the patient's head. The patient recovers, and is able to take nourishment at once.

(The Yoruba of this is probably archaic. The interpreter did not understand it, and the Babaláwo had to explain).

XIV. AJÍJA (THE DUST-DEVIL).

"Ajíja was a doctor who lived with Arámfè, and came to earth with another doctor. They made various medicines—one to kill a man when asked to do so. He pronounced certain words, and the man died. He could also kill with his walking-stick. He lives on Óke Arámfè (Óke Óra), and can only be approached through Arámfè (the father of the gods), because he is a bad man. He is worshipped near Arámfè's shrine.

"When he wishes to make trouble, he comes through the town. He sometimes sets fire to a house by picking the fire up and putting it on the thatch.

"When a man meets Ajíja, he should protect himself by putting pepper in his mouth and saying: "Ahanríyen, Fágada Shaomi" (names of Ajíja), "ki íru re bómi" (put your tail in water). The man should then spit the pepper at Ajíja.

"Sometimes Ajíja turns into a big lizard."

According to another story, Ajíja is a devil with one leg who throws men down and breaks their ankles.

www.ingramcontent.com/pod-product-compliance
Lightning Source LLC
LaVergne TN
LVHW051849080426
835512LV00018B/3164